D1523489

Patsy Mink

CHERRY LAKE PRESS

Published in the United States of America by Cherry Lake Publishing Group
Ann Arbor, Michigan
www.cherrylakepublishing.com

Reading Adviser: Beth Walker Gambro, MS, Ed., Reading Consultant, Yorkville, IL
Book Designer: Jennifer Wahi
Illustrator: Jeff Bane

Photo Credits: © SergiyN/Shutterstock, 5; © Makhh/Shutterstock, 7; © Everett Collection/Shutterstock, 9;
© Monkey Business Images/Shutterstock, 11; © fizkes/Shutterstock, 13; © Jirapong Manustrong/Shutterstock, 15,
22; © Library of Congress/Photo by Laura Patterson/LOC No. 2015645165, 17, 23; © Library of Congress/Photo by
Maureen Keeting/LOC No. 2015645194; © Library of Congress/Photo by Michael R. Jenkins/LOC No. 2021641109,
21; Jeff Bane, Cover, 1, 8, 10, 16; Various frames throughout, Shutterstock images

Cherry Lake Press is an imprint of Cherry Lake Publishing Group.

Library of Congress Cataloging-in-Publication Data

Names: Loh-Hagan, Virginia, author. | Bane, Jeff, 1957- illustrator.
Title: Patsy Mink / by Virginia Loh-Hagan ; illustrator Jeff Bane.
Description: Ann Arbor, Michigan : Cherry Lake Publishing, [2022] | Series:
   My itty-bitty bio | Audience: Grades K-1
Identifiers: LCCN 2021036745 (print) | LCCN 2021036746 (ebook) | ISBN
   9781534198975 (hardcover) | ISBN 9781668900116 (paperback) | ISBN
   9781668901557 (pdf) | ISBN 9781668905876 (ebook)
Subjects: LCSH: Mink, Patsy T., 1927-2002. | Legislators--United
   States--Biography--Juvenile literature. | Women legislators--United
   States--Biography--Juvenile literature. |
   Legislators--Hawaii--Biography--Juvenile literature. | Women
   legislators--Hawaii--Biography--Juvenile literature. | United States.
   Congress--Biography--Juvenile literature. | Japanese
   Americans--Biography--Juvenile literature. | Japanese American
   women--Biography--Juvenile literature.
Classification: LCC E840.8.M544 L64 2022 (print) | LCC E840.8.M544
   (ebook) | DDC 328.73/092 [B]--dc23
LC record available at https://lccn.loc.gov/2021036745
LC ebook record available at https://lccn.loc.gov/2021036746

Printed in the United States of America
Corporate Graphics

table of contents

About the author: When not writing, Dr. Virginia Loh-Hagan serves as the director of the Asian Pacific Islander Desi American (APIDA) Resource Center at San Diego State University. She identifies as Chinese American and is committed to amplifying APIDA communities. She lives in San Diego with her very tall husband and very naughty dogs.

About the illustrator: Jeff Bane and his two business partners own a studio along the American River in Folsom, California, home of the 1849 Gold Rush. When Jeff's not sketching or illustrating for clients, he's either swimming or kayaking in the river to relax.

My grandparents **emigrated** from Japan to Hawaii. My parents were born in Hawaii. I was born there in 1927.

My brother and I grew up on a sugar **plantation**. I saw how Asian and Native Hawaiian workers were treated. They were not treated the same as White workers.

I loved learning. I loved school. But Japanese Americans were not treated well. Things got worse. Japan attacked Pearl Harbor in Hawaii. This happened when I was 14.

Many people saw Japanese Americans as the enemy. But that didn't stop me. I took part in my first **election** in high school. I ran for class president. I won!

I graduated college. I wanted to be a doctor. Doctors go to medical schools. These schools were unfair to women. No medical school accepted me. This made me mad.

What do you want to do
when you grow up?

I graduated from law school instead. But no one hired me. I started my own law **firm**.

I wanted to change unfair laws.
I became a **U.S. representative**.
I was the first woman of color to
have this job. I inspired others.

I stood up for children. I stood up for women. I stood up for people of color. I made education better. I made laws better.

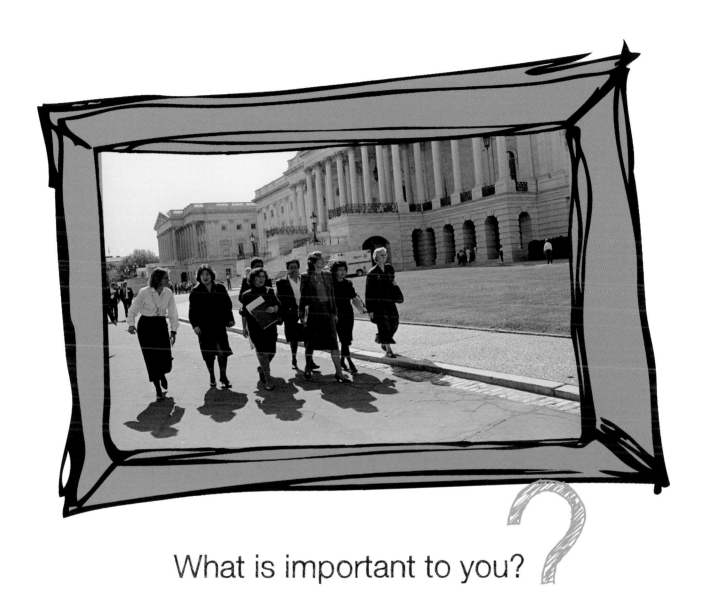

What is important to you?

I died in 2002. But my **legacy** lives on. I am known for fighting for equal rights.

What would you like to ask me?

1954

1920

Born
1927

1965

2020

Died
2002

23

glossary

election (ih-LEK-shuhn) a way people can choose their candidate or preference

emigrated (EH-muh-gray-tuhd) left one country for another

firm (FUHRM) a company or business

legacy (LEH-guh-see) something handed down from one generation to another

plantation (plan-TAY-shuhn) a large farm area where one crop is usually grown

U.S. representative (YOO ESS reh-prih-ZEN-tuh-tiv) a member of the House of Representatives in the U.S. Congress

index